BIOLOGY BASICS Need to Know

SilverTip

Food Webs

by Ruth Owen

Consultant: Jordan Stoleru
Science Educator

BEARPORT
PUBLISHING

Minneapolis, Minnesota

Credits

Cover and title page, © mel-nik/iStock; 5T, © Oleksandrum/Shutterstock; 5M, © Kurit afshen/Shutterstock; 5B, © Marcin Perkowski/Shutterstock; 7, © Utekhina Anna/Shutterstock; 8–9, © Paul Hampton/Shutterstock; 9, © Vector Tradition/Shutterstock, © Anastasiia Sorokina/Shutterstock, © OLGA 77/Shutterstock, © Rhoeo/Shutterstock, © PCH.Vector/Shutterstock, © Grafikid/Shutterstock, and © Svetlana Buzmakova/Shutterstock; 10, © EsHanPhot/Shutterstock; 11, © filmfoto/iStock; 12–13, © SJ Travel Photo and Video/Shutterstock; 14–15, © antpkr/Shutterstock; 17, © StuPorts/iStock; 18–19, © Audy39/Shutterstock; 20–21, © Deliris/Shutterstock; 23, © pamas/Shutterstock; 25, © Noel Hendrickson/Getty Images; 26–27, © graphixel/iStock; and 28, © Silver Kitten/Shutterstock, © BlueRingMedia/Shutterstock, © BlueRingMedia/Shutterstock, © Panda Vector/Shutterstock, and © VikiVector/Shutterstock.

Bearport Publishing Company Product Development Team

President: Jen Jenson; Director of Product Development: Spencer Brinker; Managing Editor: Allison Juda; Associate Editor: Naomi Reich; Associate Editor: Tiana Tran; Senior Designer: Colin O'Dea; Associate Designer: Elena Klinkner; Associate Designer: Kayla Eggert; Product Development Specialist: Anita Stasson

Library of Congress Cataloging-in-Publication Data is available at www.loc.gov or upon request from the publisher.

ISBN: 979-8-88822-036-8 (hardcover)
ISBN: 979-8-88822-228-7 (paperback)
ISBN: 979-8-88822-351-2 (ebook)

Copyright © 2024 Bearport Publishing Company. All rights reserved. No part of this publication may be reproduced in whole or in part, stored in any retrieval system, or transmitted in any form or by any means, electronic, mechanical, photocopying, recording, or otherwise, without written permission from the publisher.

For more information, write to Bearport Publishing, 5357 Penn Avenue South, Minneapolis, MN 55419.

Contents

Who's Eating Who?. 4
Energy for Life 8
Producing Power 10
The Energy Moves On 14
Around and Around 18
Bye-Bye, Producers 22
Absent Apex 24
Worldwide Webs 26

Forest Food Web .28
SilverTips for Success 29
Glossary 30
Read More 31
Learn More Online 31
Index 32
About the Author 32

Who's Eating Who?

A grasshopper munches away in a field of corn. A hungry frog watches the little insect. But before the frog can hop to its meal, a crow attacks. It snaps up the grasshopper and grabs the frog, too! In this field, it's eat or be eaten.

A cornfield isn't the only place where hungry creatures can grab a bite. This happens in ponds, gardens, forests, deserts, and more. In every **habitat**, animals feed on plants and on one another.

The animals and crops in the cornfield are part of a food web. This is a complicated system of feeding where living things eat others to survive. It connects all of the **food chains** in a place.

Food chains follow a straight line, with one creature eating another. A food web can show the many things that eat a single animal. It also shows the many things a single animal may eat.

Horses eat grass. So do sheep. Both kinds of animals eat other plants, too.

Energy for Life

As the living things within a food web eat, something very important happens. They are getting energy to grow and live. Each time an animal eats, energy is moving through the food web.

Sometimes, food webs are drawn. This helps show the movement of energy. Arrows connecting the living things show what is eaten by which things. These arrows mark how energy flows from one part of the web to another.

A Food Web

Producing Power

All food webs begin with **producers**. These living things can produce, or make, their own food. Plants are the producers in almost all food webs. How do plants get their energy? They make their own sugar for food through **photosynthesis**.

Most plants cannot eat food to get their energy. That is why they go through photosynthesis. However, there are a few plants that can get energy by eating small animals.

During photosynthesis, plants take in water from the soil. They get a gas called carbon dioxide from the air. Lastly, they need sunlight. This is a form of light energy. Plants use sunlight to turn the other ingredients into their own energy-giving food.

Photosynthesis takes place mostly in a plant's leaves. From there, the sugary food travels to the rest of the plant. It helps the producer live and grow.

The Energy Moves On

The energy from producers quickly moves on. Plant-eating animals are the next part of the web. They are called the primary, or first, **consumers**. A consumer is any animal that gets its energy by eating plants or other animals. In many food webs, grazers are the primary consumers.

> Most food webs have many consumers. They also have many producers. In a savanna habitat, first consumers include zebras, antelopes, and wildebeests. They eat many different producer plants.

Zebras are grazers in the savanna.

Often, primary consumers are also prey. They are food for meat-eating predators. These predators further along in a food web are secondary consumers. They get their energy from eating other consumers.

Within each web there are **apex predators**. Nothing hunts these top consumers.

> Some secondary consumers hunt both primary and other secondary consumers. Lions hunt primary consumer antelopes. They will also make a meal of secondary consumers hyenas and cheetahs. The lucky lions are not hunted.

The lion is an apex predator.

Around and Around

Where does a food web's energy go once it reaches an apex predator? Back to the beginning! When a top predator dies, its body becomes food.

Small **decomposers** play a big role in consuming the top consumers. They feed on rotting meat. A few larger animals eat meat from dead animals, too.

Flies lay eggs on dead bodies. Their babies hatch and then eat the meat. Molds grow over dead apex predators, too. These growths feed on consumers to take in energy.

As decomposers feed on dead bodies, they break down consumers. In time, the bodies become part of the ground. They add **nutrients** to the soil. Producers then take in those nutrients. Just like that, the food web continues.

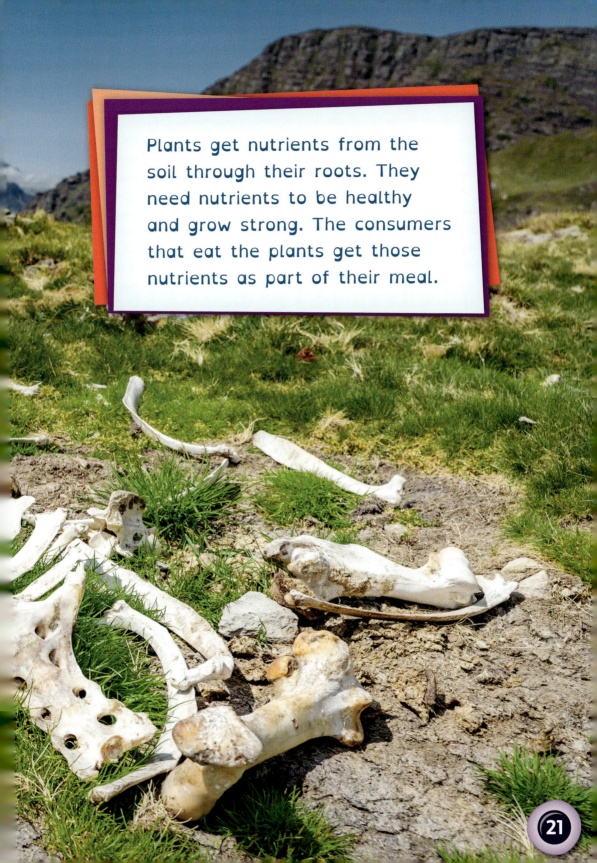

Plants get nutrients from the soil through their roots. They need nutrients to be healthy and grow strong. The consumers that eat the plants get those nutrients as part of their meal.

Bye-Bye, Producers

Food webs rely on many plants and animals to keep energy moving. So, when one living thing is lost from a food web, it can cause serious trouble.

If plants die off, the primary consumers lose their food. If primary consumers die out, secondary consumers have nothing to eat.

> When we spray chemicals on plants to kill insects, it has a bigger impact. Secondary consumers, such as birds, don't have bugs to eat. They may die.

Absent Apex

Losing an apex predator can also damage a food web. Without these predators, the numbers of primary consumers in a habitat grow. More primary consumers will eat more producers. In time, too many producers may be eaten. This leaves not enough food for many consumers in the habitat.

> Sea otters are apex predators in some food webs. They eat sea urchins. Without otters, the urchins are free to eat as much as they want. They may eat too much of a seaweed called kelp.

Worldwide Webs

All members of a food web are important. Each kind of plant or animal is a link in a chain of energy. Energy moves from small things to bigger things. It connects seaweed to sharks and grass to people. Through Earth's food webs, we are all connected.

Different food webs can become connected. A primary consumer from one web may become a secondary consumer in another. The webs soon spread far and wide.

Forest Food Web

A forest food web includes producers, primary and secondary consumers, apex predators, and decomposers. Let's look at part of a forest food web!

SilverTips for SUCCESS

★ SilverTips for REVIEW

Review what you've learned. Use the text to help you.

Define key terms

apex predator
decomposer
primary consumer
producer
secondary consumer

Check for understanding

How do producers get their energy?

What is the difference between a primary and secondary consumer?

Explain how apex predators are a part of the food web.

Think deeper

How would the food web change without one of the consumers you have in the place that you live?

★ SilverTips on TEST-TAKING

- **Make a study plan.** Ask your teacher what the test is going to cover. Then, set aside time to study a little bit every day.

- **Read all the questions carefully.** Be sure you know what is being asked.

- **Skip any questions** you don't know how to answer right away. Mark them and come back later if you have time.

Glossary

apex predators animals that are not hunted by any other animals

consumers the living things that eat other things in a food web

decomposers the living things that break down dead plants and the bodies of dead animals

food chains series of plants and animals that depend on one another for food

habitat a place in nature where plants and animals live

nutrients things needed by plants and animals to grow and stay healthy

photosynthesis the process of making food using water, carbon dioxide, and sunlight

producers things in a food web that are able to make their own food

Read More

Gunasekara, Mignonne. *Killer Mammals (Predators on the Prowl).* New York: Gareth Stevens Publishing, 2022.

Huddleston, Emma. *Decomposers and Scavengers: Nature's Recyclers (Team Earth).* Minneapolis: Abdo Publishing, 2020.

Jacobson, Bray. *Food Chains and Webs (A Look at Nature's Cycles).* New York: Gareth Stevens Publishing, 2020.

Learn More Online

1. Go to **www.factsurfer.com** or scan the QR code below.
2. Enter "**Food Webs**" into the search box.
3. Click on the cover of this book to see a list of websites.

Index

animals 4, 6–7, 10, 14, 18, 22, 26

apex predators 16–19, 24, 28

decomposers 18, 20, 28

food chain 6

habitats 4, 14, 24

nutrients 20–21

photosynthesis 10, 12

plants 4, 7, 10, 12, 14, 21–22, 26

predators 16–19, 24, 28

prey 16

primary consumer 14, 16, 22, 24, 26, 28

producers 10, 12, 14, 20, 22, 24, 28

secondary consumer 16, 22, 26, 28

About the Author

Ruth Owen has been making books for more than 12 years. She lives in Cornwall, England, just minutes from the ocean. Ruth loves to write books about nature.